WILLIAM SHAKESPEARE
TWELFTH NIGHT

Illustrated by John H. Howard

OVAL PROJECTS LIMITED
SIDGWICK & JACKSON LIMITED

Published by Oval Projects Limited
335 Kennington Road, London SE11 4QE

British Library Cataloguing in Publication Data
Shakespeare, William
    Twelfth Night.
    I. Title   II. Gibson, David
    III. Howard, John
    822.3 PR2837

ISBN 0 283 99132 1 hardcover
ISBN 0 283 99136 4 softcover

Edited by David Gibson, London
Series design by Jim Wire, Folkestone, Kent
Lettering by Steve Craddock and June Sinclair

Origination by Columbia Offset, Singapore
Printed by Mandarin Offset (HK) Limited
Hong Kong

Distributed by Sidgwick & Jackson Limited
1 Tavistock Chambers, Bloomsbury Way
London WC1A 2SG

THE STORY

Count **Orsino,** the ruler of an imaginary country called Illyria, is madly in love with the Countess **Olivia.** But Olivia is in mourning for her brother and will have nothing to do with Orsino. Olivia has to put up with **Sir Toby Belch,** her uncle, and **Feste,** the court jester she inherited from her father. Sir Toby is busy encouraging his wealthy friend **Sir Andrew Aguecheek** to court Olivia. Sir Toby and Sir Andrew spend a good deal of time getting drunk together with Sir Andrew paying for the drinks.

Into this story comes **Viola.** She has been washed up on the shores of Illyria after a shipwreck. She believes her identical twin brother, **Sebastian,** has been drowned. Viola decides to dress up as a boy and enter the service of Orsino. She takes the name Cesario, and becomes Orsino's page. The Count is very taken with the new 'boy' and sends Cesario to woo Olivia on his behalf. The plan backfires when Olivia falls for Cesario.

Malvolio, who runs Olivia's household, disapproves of Sir Toby, Sir Andrew, and **Maria,** Olivia's maid. To get their own back they arrange for Malvolio to think that Olivia is in love with him. While strolling in the garden Malvolio finds a letter, apparently from Olivia, but in fact forged by Maria. He carefully follows the weird instructions given in the letter. Olivia finds Malvolio's behaviour so strange that she believes he is mad and asks Sir Toby to look after him. Instead Sir Toby and the others lock up Malvolio and torment him.

Sir Andrew discovers Olivia's passion for Cesario, and announces he is going to give up all hope of her. Sir Toby and **Fabian** convince him she is only flirting with Cesario to make him jealous. They incite him to challenge Cesario to a duel. Neither Sir Andrew nor Viola, as Cesario, are keen to fight and try hard to avoid each other.

In the meantime, the lost twin, **Sebastian,** has turned up in Illyria. He is convinced that Viola was lost in the shipwreck. With him is **Antonio,** the ship's captain who rescued him. Sebastian wants to go sight-seeing but Antonio, who is a wanted man in Illyria, has to keep out of the way. They part having agreed to meet later at their hotel. Antonio then bumps into Viola. Mistaking her for Sebastian he saves her from the fight with Sir Andrew. But he is recognised by the police and arrested.

Sebastian runs into Sir Toby and Sir Andrew. They mistake him for Cesario and try to pick a fight with him. Olivia interrupts them, and assuming Sebastian to be Cesario, she invites him home. Never having seen this woman in his life, Sebastian is surprised, but accepts anyway. They are later secretly married.

Orsino has grown tired of the lack of progress he is making with Olivia and arrives at her mansion with his entourage, including Viola. Olivia reveals to Orsino that she and Cesario are married. Viola, as Cesario, denies it. Sir Toby and Sir Andrew appear, wounded from another fight with Sebastian. Sebastian himself joins the assembled company and comes face to face with Viola. The identity puzzle is solved.

Olivia is not at all put out at having married the wrong person, and Orsino quickly accepts that Cesario is in fact Viola, and proposes to her. Sir Toby and Maria, flushed with the success of having made a fool of Malvolio, have also wed. Malvolio is finally released. He is told about the joke that has been played on him and is not amused.

Everybody goes off to celebrate their good fortune, except Malvolio who is left out in the cold. Feste, also alone, laments in a song how silly everything and everyone is.

1

Will you go hunt, my lord?

What, Curio?

The hart.[A]

Why so I do: the noblest that I have.

O, when mine eyes did see Olivia first, methought she purged the air of pestilence.

That instant was I turned into a hart, and my desires, like fell and cruel hounds, e'er since pursue me.

Enter Valentine

How now! What news from her?

So please my lord, I might not be admitted, but from her handmaid do return this answer:

The element itself, till seven years' heat, shall not behold her face at ample view, but like a cloistress she will veilèd walk, and water once a day her chamber round with eye-offending brine; all this to season a brother's dead love, which she would keep fresh and lasting, in her sad remembrance.

O, she that hath a heart of that fine frame to pay this debt of love but to a brother— how will she love, when the rich golden shaft[A] hath killed the flock of all affections else that live in her; when liver,[A] brain and heart, these sovereign thrones, are all supplied and filled —her sweet perfections— with one self king!

Away before me to sweet beds of flowers! Love-thoughts lie rich when canopied with bowers.

It is perchance that you yourself were saved.

O, my poor brother! And so perchance may he be!

True, madam.

And to comfort you with chance, assure yourself after our ship did split, when you and those poor number saved with you hung on our driving boat,

I saw your brother, most provident in peril, bind himself—courage and hope both teaching him the practice—to a strong mast that lived upon the sea; where, like Arion on the dolphin's back, I saw him hold acquaintance with the waves so long as I could see.

For saying so, there's gold.

Mine own escape unfoldeth to my hope, whereto thy speech serves for authority, the like of him.

Knowest thou this country?

Ay, madam, well, for I was bred and born not three hours' travel from this very place.

Who governs here?

A noble Duke, in nature as in name.

What is his name?

Orsino.

Good Mistress Mary Accost...

You mistake, knight. 'Accost' is front her, board her, woo her, assail her!

By my troth, I would not undertake her in this company. Is that the meaning of 'accost'?

Fare you well, gentlemen.

An thou let part so, Sir Andrew, would thou mightst never draw sword again.

An you part so, mistress, I would I might never draw sword again.

Fair lady, do you think you have fools in hand?

Sir, I have not you by the hand.

Marry, but you shall have, and here's my hand.

Now, sir, 'Thought is free'. I pray you, bring your hand to the ᴬ buttery bar ᴬ and let it drink.

Wherefore, sweetheart? What's your metaphor?

It's dry⁺, sir.

Why, I think so. I am not such an ass but I can keep my hand dry.

But what's your jest?

A dry jest⁺, sir.

Are you full of them?

Ay, sir. I have them at my fingers' ends.

Marry, now I let go your hand, I am barren⁺.

I am a fellow o'the strangest mind i'the world. I delight in masques and revels sometimes altogether.

Art thou good at these kickshawses,* knight?

As any man in Illyria, whatsoever he be, under the degree of my betters.

And yet I will not compare with an old man.*

What is thy excellence in a galliard,* knight?

Faith, I can cut a caper.*

And I can cut the mutton to't.

And I think I have the back-trick* simply as strong as any man in Illyria.

Wherefore are these things hid? Wherefore have these gifts a curtain before 'em? Are they like to take dust, like *Mistress Mall's picture? Why dost thou not go to church in a galliard and come home in a coranto?*

My very walk should be a jig!

I would not so much as make water but in a sink-a-pace.*

What dost thou mean? Is it a world to hide virtues in? I did think by the excellent constitution of thy leg, it was formed under the star of a galliard.*

Ay, 'tis strong, and it does indifferent well in a dun*-coloured stock.

Shall we set about some revels?

What shall we do else?

Were we not born under *Taurus?

Taurus?

That's sides and heart.

No, sir! It is legs and thighs!

Let me see thee caper!

Ha! Higher! Ha! Ha!

Excellent!

ACT I, SCENE IV: ORSINO'S HOUSE

Enter Viola, disguised as a man, and Valentine

If the Duke continue these favours towards you, Cesario, you are like to be much advanced. He hath known you but three days, and already you are no stranger.

You either fear his humour or my negligence, that you call in question the continuance of his love. Is he inconstant, sir, in his favours?

No, believe me.

Enter Orsino, Curio and attendants

I thank you.

Here comes the Count.

Who saw Cesario, ho?

On your attendance, my lord, here!

Stand you awhile aloof.

Cesario, thou knowest no less but all. I have unclasped to thee the book even of my secret soul.

Be clamorous and leap all civil bounds rather than make unprofited return.

Therefore, good youth, address thy gait unto her. Be not denied access; stand at her doors, and tell them there thy fixèd foot shall grow till thou have audience.

Sure, my noble lord, if she be so abandoned to her sorrow as it is spoke, she never will admit me.

May, either tell me where thou hast been, or I will not open my lips so wide as a bristle may enter, in way of thy excuse. My lady will hang thee for thy absence.

Let her hang me. He that is well hanged in this world needs to fear no colours.*

Make that good.

He shall see none to fear.

A good lenten answer!*

I can tell thee where that saying was born, of 'I fear no colours'.

Where, good Mistress Mary?

In the wars.

And that may you be bold to say in your foolery.

Well, God give them wisdom that have it; and those that are fools, let them use their talents.

Yet you will be hanged for being so long absent; or to be turned away — is not that as good as a hanging to you?

Many a good hanging prevents a bad marriage; and for turning away — let summer bear it out.*

You are resolute, then?

...t so neither, but I am resolved ...two points.*

That if one break, the other will hold.

Or if both break, your gaskins* fall!

Apt, in good faith, very apt.

Well, go thy way.

If Sir Toby would leave drinking, thou wert as witty a piece of Eve's flesh as any in Illyria.*

Peace, you rogue, no more o'that.

Here comes my lady.

Make your excuse wisely, you were best.

Can you do it?

Dexteriously, good madonna.

Make your proof.

I must catechize you for it, madonna. Good my mouse of virtue, answer me.

Well, sir, for want of other idleness, I'll bide your proof.

Good madonna, why mourn'st thou?

Good fool, for my brother's death.

I think his soul is in hell, madonna.

I know his soul is in heaven, fool.

The more fool, madonna, to mourn your brother's soul, being in heaven.

Take away the fool, gentlemen!

What think you of this fool, Malvolio? Doth he not mend?^

Yes, and shall do, till the pangs of death shake him.

Infirmity, that decays the wise, doth ever make the better fool.

God send you, sir, a speedy infirmity, for the better increasing your folly.

Sir Toby will be sworn that I am no fox^ but he will not pass his word for twopence that you are no fool.

How say you to that, Malvolio?

I marvel your ladyship takes delight in such a barren rascal. I saw him put down the other day with an ordinary fool, that has no more brain than a stone.

Look you now, he's out of his guard already; unless you laugh and minister occasion to him, he is gagged.

protest I take these wise men, that crow so these set kind of fools, no better than the ools' zanies.^

O, you are sick of self-love, Malvolio, and taste with a distempered appetite.

To be generous, guiltless and of free disposition, is to take those things for birdbolts^ that you deem cannon bullets.

There is no slander in an allowed fool, though he do nothing but rail; nor no railing in a known discreet man, though he do nothing but reprove.

Now Mercury^ endue thee with leasing^ for thou speak'st well of fools!

Madam, there is at the gate a young gentleman much desires to speak with you.

From the Count Orsino, is it?

I know not, madam. Tis a fair young man, and well attended.

Who of my people hold him in delay?

Sir Toby, madam, your kinsman.

Fetch him off, I pray you; he speaks nothing but madman!

Fie on him!

Are you the lady of the house?

If I do not usurp myself,△ I am.

Most certain, if you are she, you do usurp yourself;△ for what is yours to bestow is not yours to reserve.△

But this is from my commission. I will on with my speech in your praise, and then show you the heart of my message.

Come to what is important in't. I forgive you the praise.

Alas, I took great pains to study it, and 'tis poetical.

It is the more like to be feigned; I pray you, keep it in.

I heard you were saucy at my gates, and allowed your approach rather to wonder at you than to hear you. If you be mad, be gone; if you have reason, be brief.

'Tis not that time of moon with me, to make one in so skipping a dialogue.

Will you hoist sail, sir?

Here lies your way.

No, good swabber,△ I am to hull△ here a little longer.

Some mollification for your giant,△ sweet lady.

Tell me your mind; I am a messenger.

Sure, you have some hideous matter to deliver, when the courtesy of it is so fearful.

Speak your office.

It alone concerns your ear. I bring no overture of war, no taxation of homage.

I hold the olive in my hand; my words are as full of peace as matter.

Yet you began rudely.

What are you?

What would you?

The rudeness that hath appeared in me have I learned from my entertainment.

What I am and what I would are as secret as maidenhead; to your ears — divinity, to any other's — profanation.

Give us the place alone.
We will hear this divinity.

Now, sir, what is your text?

Most sweet lady —

A comfortable doctrine,
and much may be said of it.

Where lies your text?

In Orsino's bosom.

In his bosom!
In what chapter
of his bosom?

To answer by
the method:
in the first
of his heart.

O, I have read it;
it is heresy.

Have you no
more to say?

Good
madam,
let me
see your
face.

Have you any commission
from your lord to negotiate
with my face? You are now
out of your text.

But we will draw the curtain
and show you the picture.

Look you, sir, such a
one I was this present.

Is't not well done?

Excellently done —
if God did all.

'Tis in grain, sir;
'twill endure
wind and weather.

30

Here comes the fool, i'faith!

How now, my hearts?

Did you never see the picture of *We Three*?

WE THREE

By my troth, the fool has an excellent breast I had rather than forty shillings I had such a leg, and so sweet a breath to sing, as the fool has!

Welcome, ass!

Now let's have a catch!

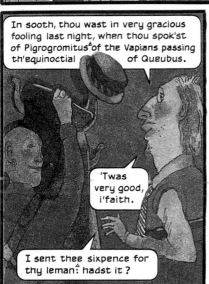

In sooth, thou wast in very gracious fooling last night, when thou spok'st of Pigrogromitus of the Vapians passing th'equinoctial of Queubus.

'Twas very good, i'faith.

I sent thee sixpence for thy leman: hadst it ?

I did *impeticos* thy *gratillity*, for Malvolio's nose is no whipstock, my lady has a white hand, and the Myrmidons are no bottle-ale houses.

Excellent! Why, this is the best fooling, when all is done!

Now, a song!

Come on, there sixpence for yo Let's have a son

And there's a testril of me too. If one knight give a —

Would you have a love-song or a song of good life ?

A love-song, a love-song!

Ay, ay. I care not for good life

O mistress mine, where are you roaming?
O, stay and hear your true love's coming,
That can sing both high and low.
Trip no further, pretty sweeting;
Journeys end in lovers' meeting,
Every wise man's son doth know.

Excellent good, i'faith.

Good, good.

What is love? 'Tis not hereafter;
Present mirth hath present laughter,
What's to come is still unsure.
In delay there lies no plenty,
Then come kiss me, sweet and twenty,
Youth's a stuff will not endure.

A mellifluous voice, as I am a true knight!

A contagious breath!

Very sweet and contagious, i'faith.

To hear by the nose, it is dulcet in contagion.

But shall we make the welkin dance indeed? Shall we rouse the night-owl in a catch that will draw three souls out of one weaver?

Shall we do that?

An you love me, lets do't!

I am dog at a catch!

By'r lady, sir, and some dogs will catch well.

Most certain!

Let our catch be 'Thou knave'!

'Hold thy peace, thou knave', knight? I shall be constrained in't to call thee 'knave', knight.

'Tis not the first time I have constrained one to call me knave!

Begin, fool! It begins 'Hold thy peace!'

I shall never begin if I hold my peace!

Good, i'faith!

Come, begin.

What a caterwauling do you keep here! If my lady have not called up her steward Malvolio and bid him turn you out of doors, never trust me!

My lady's a ... Cataian; we are ... politicians; Malvolio's a Peg-a-Ramsey; and — Three merry men be we!

Am not I consanguineous? Am I not of her blood?

Tilly-vally! "Lady"!

There dwelt a man in Babylon, Lady!

'Lady!'

Beshrew me, the knight's in admirable fooling.

Ay, he does well enough if he be disposed, and so do I too. He does it with a better grace, but I do it more natural.

O'the twelfth day of December—!

For the love o'God, peace!

My masters, are you mad? Or what are you?

Have you no wit, manners nor honesty, but to gabble like tinkers at this time of night?

Do ye make an alehouse of my lady's house, that ye squeak out your coziers'*catches without any mitigation or remorse of voice?

Is there no respect of place, persons, nor time in you?

We did keep time, sir, in our catches. Sneck up!*

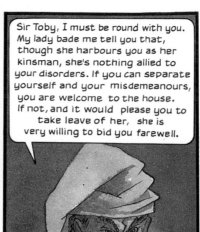

Sir Toby, I must be round with you. My lady bade me tell you that, though she harbours you as her kinsman, she's nothing allied to your disorders. If you can separate yourself and your misdemeanours, you are welcome to the house. If not, and it would please you to take leave of her, she is very willing to bid you farewell.

Farewell, dear heart, since I must needs be gone!

Nay, good Sir Toby!

His eye do show his days are almo done!

Is't even so!

But I will never die!

Sir Toby, there you lie!

This is much credit to you!

Shall I bid him go?

What an if you do?

Shall I bid him go, and spare no

Oh no, no, no, no, you dare not

Out o'tune, sir?

Ye lie!

Art any more than a steward?

Dost thou think because thou art virtuous, there shall be no more cakes and ale?

Yes, by Saint Anne, and ginger* shall be hot i'the mouth too!

Th'art i'the righ

39

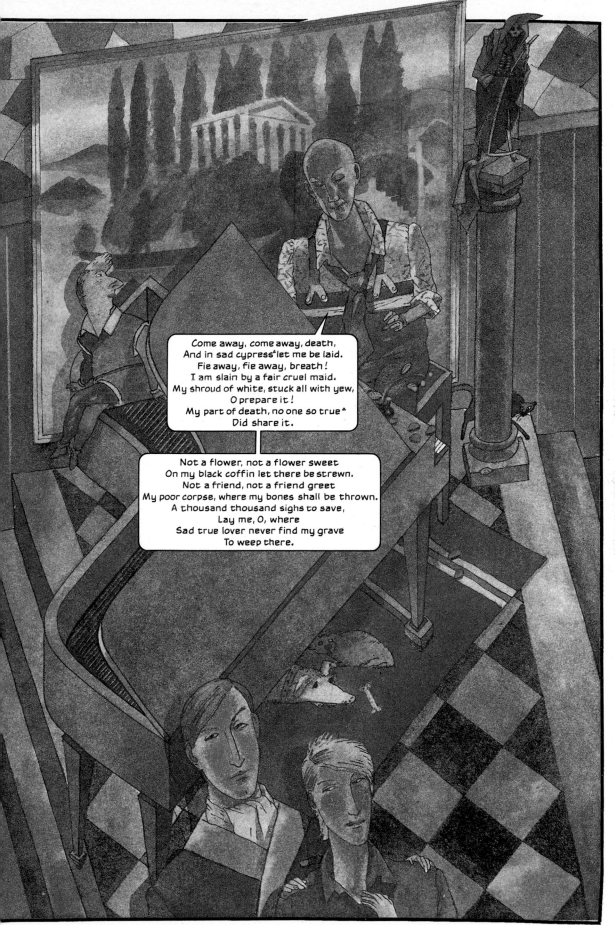

To be *Count* Malvolio...

Ah, rogue!

Pistol him, pistol him!

Peace, peace!

There is example for't. The Lady of the Strachy[△] married the yeoman of the wardrobe.

Fie on him! Jezebel![△]

O, peace!

Now he's deeply in. Look how imagination blows[△] him.

Having been three months married to her, sitting in my state...

O for a stone-bow[△] to hit him in the eye!

Calling my officers about me, in my branchèd[△] velvet gown, having come from a day-bed where I have left Olivia sleeping...

Fire and brimstone!

O peace, peace!

And then to have the humour of state; and after a demure travel of regard[△] – telling them I know my place as I would they should do theirs – to ask for my kinsman Toby!

Bolts and shackles!

O peace, peace, peace Now, now!

53

55

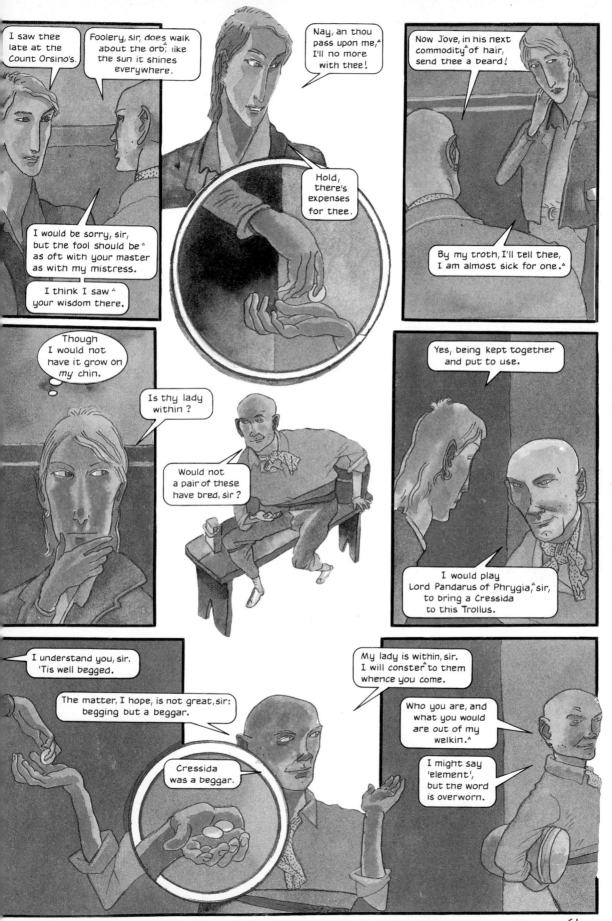

61

This fellow is wise enough to play the fool; and to do that well craves^ a kind of wit. He must observe their mood on whom he jests, the quality of persons, and the time, and, like the haggard,^ check at every feather that comes before his eye.

This is a practice as full of labour as a wise man's art. For folly that he wisely shows is fit; but wise men, folly-fall'n,^ quite taint their wit.

Save you, gentleman.

And you, sir.

Dieu vous garde, Monsieur.

Et vous aussi: votre serviteur.

I hope, sir, you are, and I am yours.

Will you encounter the house? My niece is desirous you should enter, if your trade be to her.

I am bound to your niece, sir.

I mean, she is the list^ of my voyage.

Taste your legs, sir; put them to motion.

My legs do better understand me, sir, than I understand what you mean by bidding me taste my legs.

I mean to go, sir: to enter.

I will answer you with gait and entrance.

But we are prevented!^

Most excellent accomplished lady, the heavens rain odours on you!

That youth's a rare courtier: 'rain odours' — well!

My matter hath no voice, lady, but to your own most pregnant^and vouchsafèd ear.

'odours',

'pregnant',

and 'vouchsafèd'!

I'll get 'em all three all ready!^

Let the garden door be shut, and leave me to my hearing.

Give me your hand, sir.

My duty, madam, and most humble service.

What is your name?

ACT III, SCENE II: OLIVIA'S HOUSE

No, faith, I'll not stay a jot longer!

You must needs yield your reason, Sir Andrew.

Thy reason, dear venom, give thy reason.

Marry, I saw your niece do more favours to the Count's serving-man than ever she bestowed upon me.

I saw't i'th' orchard.

Did she see thee the while, old boy? Tell me that.

As plain as I see you now.

This was a great argument of love in her toward you.

'Slight! Will you make an ass of me?

I will prove it legitimate, sir, upon the oaths of judgement and reason.

And they have been grand-jurymen since before Noah was a sailor.

Challenge me the Count's youth to fight with him! Hurt him in eleven places!

My niece shall take note of it; and assure thyself there is no love-broker in the world can more prevail in man's commendation with woman than report of valour.

There is no way but this, Sir Andrew.

Will either of you bear me a challenge to him?

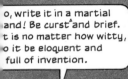

o, write it in a martial and! Be curst[a] and brief. t is no matter how witty, o it be eloquent and full of invention.

Taunt him with the licence of ink![a]

If thou thou'st him some thrice, it shall not be amiss; and as many lies as will lie in thy sheet of paper— although the sheet were big enough for the bed of Ware in England[a]— set 'em down!

Go! About it!

Let there be gall[a] enough in thy ink, though thou write with a goose pen,[a] no matter! About it!

Where shall I find you?

We'll call thee at thy cubiculo![a]

Go!

72

Th'offence is not of such a bloody nature — albeit the quality of the time and quarrel might well have given us bloody argument.

It might have since been answered in repaying what we took from them — which for traffic's sake,^ most of our city did.

Only myself stood out!

For which, if I be lapsèd^ in this place, I shall pay dear.

Do not then walk too open.

It doth not fit me.

Hold, sir: here's my purse.

In the south suburbs, at the Elephant,^ is best to lodge.

I will bespeak our diet,^ whiles you beguile the time and feed your knowledge with viewing of the town.

There shall you have me.

Why I your purse?

ply your eye shall light upon me toy you have desire to rchase : and your store, I ink, is not for idle markets,^ sir.

I'll be your purse-bearer, and leave you for an hour.

To th'Elephant.

I do remember.

How now, Malvolio?

Sweet lady!

Ho!

Ho!

Smil'st thou?

I sent for thee upon a sad occasion.

Sad, lady? I could be sad: this does make some obstruction in the blood— this *cross-gartering!*

But what of that?

If it please the eye of *one*, it is with me as the very true sonnet is: *'please one, and please all'*

Why, how dost thou, man? What is the matter with thee?

Not black in my mind,

though yellow in my legs!

It did come to his hands, and commands shall be executed.

I think we do know the sweet Roman hand^...

Wilt thou go to bed, Malvolio?

To bed?

Ay, sweetheart, and I'll come to thee!

God comfort thee! Why dost thou smile so, and kiss thy hand so oft?

How do you, Malvolio?

At your request!

Yes, nightingales answer daws!*

Why appear you with this ridiculous boldness before my lady?

'Be not afraid of greatness': 'twas well writ.

What mean'st thou by that Malvolio?

75

'Some are born great' —

Ha?

'Some achieve greatness' —

What sayst thou?

'And some have greatness thrust upon them'.

Heaven restore thee!

'Remember who commended thy yellow stockings'.

Thy yellow stockings?

'And wished to see thee cross-gartered'.

Cross-gartered?

'Go to, thou art made, if thou desir'st to be so'.

Am I maid!

'If not, let me see thee a servant still'.

Why this is ver midsummer madness!

Madam, the young gentleman of the Count Orsino is returned; I could hardly entreat him back. He attends your ladyship's pleasure.

I'll come to him.

Good Maria, let this fellow be looked to.

Where's my Cousin Toby?

Let some of my people have a special care of him.

I would not have him miscarry for the half of my dowry.

How is't with you, sir? How is't with you, man?

Go off, I discard you. Let me enjoy my private. Go off.

Lo, how hollow the fiend speaks within him! Did not I tell you?

Sir Toby, my lady prays you to have a care of him.

Aha! Does she so?

Go to, go to. Peace, peace, we must deal gently with him. Let me alone.

How do you, Malvolio? How is't with you? What, man, defy the devil! Consider, he's an enemy to mankind.

Do you know what you say?

La you, an you speak ill of the devil, how he takes it at heart! Pray God he be not bewitched.

Carry his water to th'wisewoma

Marry, and it shall be done tomorrow morning, if I live!

My lady would not lose him for more than I'll say!

How now, mistress?

O Lord!

Prithee, hold thy peace, this is not the way. Do you not see you move him? Let me alone with him.

No way but gentlenes gently, gently. The fier is rough, and will not be roughly used.

78

Why, how now, my bawcock^? How dost thou, chuck?

Sir!

Ay, biddy, come with me.

What, man, 'tis not for gravity^ to play at ^cherry-pit with Satan! Hang him, foul collier!^

Get him to say his prayers, good Sir Toby. get him to pray!

No, I warrant you, he will not hear of godliness!

My prayers, minx!

Go, hang yourselves all! You are idle, shallow things! I am not of your element.

You shall know more hereafter.

Is't possible?

His very genius^hath taken the infection of the device, man!

If this were played upon a stage now, I could condemn it as an improbable fiction!

Nay, pursue him now, lest the device take air,^ and taint!

Why, we shall make him mad indeed!

The house will be the quieter.

Come, we'll have him in a dark room, and bound!

My niece is already in the belief that he's mad: we may carry it thus for our pleasure and his penance, till our very pastime, tired out of breath, prompt us to have mercy on him.

At which time we will bring the device to the bar,^ and crown thee for a finder of madmen.

But see, but see!

79

More matter for a May morning!

Here's the challenge. Read it: I warrant there's vinegar and pepper in't.

Is't so saucy?

Ay, is't, I warrant him. Do but read.

Give me.

Youth, whatsoever thou art, thou art but a scurvy fellow.

Good, and valiant.

Wonder not, nor admire not in thy mind why I do call thee so, for I will show thee no reason for't.

A good note, that keeps you from the blow of the law.

Thou com'st to the Lady Olivia, and in my sight she uses thee kindly: but thou liest in thy throat; that is not the matter I challenge thee for.

Very brief, and to exceeding good sense —

—less.

I will waylay thee going home, where if it be thy chance to kill me —

Good.

Thou kill'st me like a rogue and a villain.

Still you keep o'th'windy side of the law. Good.

Fare thee well, and God have mercy on one of our souls! He may have mercy upon mine, but my hope is better, and so look to thyself!

Thy friend, as thou usest him, and thy sworn enemy,

Andrew Aguecheek.

If this letter move him not, his legs cannot. I'll give't him.

You may have very fit occasion for't: he is now in some commerce with my lady, and will by and by depart.

Go, Sir Andrew: scout me for him at the corner of the orchard, like a bum-baily.*

So soon as ever thou see'st him, draw, and as thou draw'st, swear horrible: for it comes to pass oft that a terrible oath, with a swaggering accent sharply twanged off, gives manhood more approbation than ever proof itself would have earned him.

Away!

Nay, let me alone for swearing.*

Now will not I deliver his letter, for the behaviour of the young gentleman gives him out to be of good capacity and breeding: his employment between his lord and my niece confirms no less.

Therefore, this letter, being so excellently ignorant, will breed no terror in the youth: he will find it comes from a clodpole.*

But, sir, I will deliver his challenge by word of mouth, set upon Aguecheek a notable report of valour, and drive the gentleman (as I know his youth will aptly receive it) into a most hideous opinion of his rage, skill, fury, and impetuosity.

...his will so fright ...em both that they ...ill kill one another by the look —

...ke cockatrices!*

Here he comes with your niece: give them way till he take leave, and presently after him.

I will meditate the while upon some horrid message for a challenge.

81

There's no remedy, sir; he will fight with you for oath's sake.

Marry, he hath better bethought him of his quarrel, and he finds that now scarce to be worth talking of.

Therefore draw, for the supportance of his vow.ˆ

He protests he will not hurt you.

Pray God defend me.

A little thing would make me tell them how much I lack of a man.

Give ground if you see him furious.

Come, Sir Andre there's no reme

The gentleman will, for his honour's sake, have one bout with you. He cannot, by the *duello*ˆavoid it. But he has promised me, as he is a gentleman and a soldier, he will not hurt you.

Come on. To't!

Pray God he keep his oath!

Enter Antonio

I do assure you, 'tis against my will.

Put up your sword!

If this young gentleman have done offence, I take the fault on me. If you offend him, I for him defy you!

You, Sir? Why, what are you?

One, sir, that for his love dares yet do more than you hav heard him brag to you he will.

Nay, if you be an undertaker, I am for you!

O, good Sir Toby, hold! Here come the Officers!

I'll be with you anon!

Pray, sir, put your sword up, if you please.

Marry, will I, sir. And for that I promised you, I'll be as good as my word. He will bear you easily, and reins well.

This is the man. Do thy office.

Antonio, I arrest thee at the suit of Count Orsino.

You do mistake me, sir.

No, sir, no jot. I know your favour well though now you have no sea-cap on your head.

Take him away. He knows I know him well.

I must obey.

This comes with seeking you. But there's no remedy: I shall answer it.

What will you do, now my necessity makes me to ask you for my purse?

It grieves me much more for what I cannot do for you than what befalls myself.

You stand amazed, but be of comfort.

Come, sir, away!

I must entreat of you some of that money.

What money, sir?

For the fair kindness you have showed me here, and part being prompted by your present trouble, out of my lean and low ability I'll lend you something.

My having is not much. I'll make division of my present with you.

Hold, there's half my coffer.

Do not tempt my misery, lest that it makes me so unsound a man as to upbraid you with those kindnesses that I have done for you.

I hate ingratitude more in a man than lying, vainness, babbling drunkenness or any taint of vice whose strong corruption inhabits our frail blood.

O heavens themselves!

Come sir, I pray you go.

Will you deny me now?

Is't possible that my deserts to you can lack persuasion?

I know of none, nor know I you by voice or any feature.

I my brother know yet living in my glass.

He named Sebastian!

Even such and so in favour was my brother.

And he went still in this fashion, colour, ornament, for him I imitate!

O if it prove, tempest are kind, and s[ea] waves fresh in love!

A very dishonest, paltry boy, and more a coward than a hare! His dishonesty appears in leaving his friend here in necessity, and denying him; and for his cowardship, ask Fabian.

A coward, a most devout coward! Religious in it!

'Slid, I'll after him again, and beat him!

Do, cuff him soundly!

But never draw thy sword!

An I do not — !

Come, let's see the event!

I dare lay any mone[y] 'twill be nothing ye[t]

ACT IV, SCENE I:
OUTSIDE
OLIVIA'S HOUSE.
Feste & Sebastian.

Will you make me believe that I am not sent for you?

Go to, go to, thou art a foolish fellow! Let me be clear of thee!

Well held out, i'faith!

No, I do not know you, nor I am not sent to you by my lady to bid you come speak with her, nor your name is not Master Cesario!

Nor this is not my nose neither!

Nothing that is so, is so!

I prithee vent thy folly somewhere else; thou know'st not me!

Vent my folly! He has heard that word of some great man and now applies it to a fool.

Vent my folly?

I am afraid this great lubber, the world will prove a cockney!

I prithee now, *ungird thy strangeness*, and tell me what I shall *vent* to my lady.

Shall I *vent* to her that thou art coming?

I prithee, foolish Greek, depart from me.

There's money for thee.

If you tarry longer, I shall give worse payment.

By my troth, thou hast an open hand.

These wise men that give fools money get themselves a good report —

—after fourteen years' purchase!

95

Well, I'll put it on, and I will dissemble myself in't. And I would I were the first that ever dissembled in such a gown. I am not tall enough to become the function well, nor lean enough to be thought a good student; but to be said an honest man and a good housekeeper goes as fairly as to say a careful man and a great scholar.

The competitors enter!

Jove bless thee, Master Parson!

Bonos dies,[△] Sir Toby!

For as the old hermit of Prague,[△] that never saw pen and ink, very wittily said to a niece of King Gorboduc, 'That that is, is'. So I, being Master Parson, *am* Master Parson — for what is *'that'* but *'that'*, and *'is'* but *'is'*?

To him, Sir Topas!

What ho, I say! Peace in this prison!

The knave counterfeits well! A good knave!

Who calls there?

Sir Topas the curate, who comes to visit Malvolio the lunatic.

Sir Topas, Sir Topas, good Sir Topas! Go to my lady!

Out, hyperbolical fiend! How vexest thou this man! Talk'st thou nothing but of ladies?

Well said, Master Parson.

Sir Topas, never was man thus wronged! Good Sir Topas, do not think I am mad. They have laid me here in hideous darkness!

Fie, thou dishonest Satan!

I call thee by the most modest terms, for I am one of those gentle ones that will use the devil himself with courtesy.

Sayest thou that house is dark?

As hell, Sir Topas!

Why, it hath bay windows transparent as barricadoes,[a] and the clerestories[a] toward the south-north are as lustrous[a] as ebony!

And yet complainst thou of obstruction?

I am not mad, Sir Topas. I say to you, this house is dark.

Madman, thou errest!

I say there is no darkness but ignorance, in which thou art more puzzled than th'Egyptians in their fog.[a]

I say this house is dark as ignorance, though ignorance were as dark as hell. And I say there was never man thus abused.

I am no more mad than you are!

Make the trial of it in any constant question.

What is the opinion of Pythagoras[A] concerning wildfowl?

That the soul of our grandam might haply inhabit a bird.

What thinkest thou of his opinion?

I think nobly of the soul, and no way approve his opinion.

Fare thee well. Remain thou still in darkness. Thou shalt hold the opinion of Pythagoras ere I will allow of thy wits, and fear to kill a woodcock lest thou dispossess the soul of thy grandam! Fare thee well.

Sir Topas, Sir Topas!

My most exquisite Sir Topas!

Nay, I am for all waters![A]

Thou might'st have done this without thy beard and gown: he sees thee not.

To him in thine own voice and bring me word how thou find'st him.

I would we were well rid of this knavery.

If he may be conveniently delivered, I would he were, for I am now so far in offence with my niece that I cannot pursue with any safety this sport to the upshot.

Come by and by to my chamber.

Ay, good fool.

Alas, sir, how fell you besides your five wits?[A]

Fool, there was never man so notoriously abused! I am as well in my wits, fool, as thou art.

But as well? Then you are mad indeed, if you be no better in your wits than a fool!

They have here propertied[A] me: keep me in darkness, send ministers to me — asses! — and do all they can to face me out of my wits.

Advise you what you say: the minister is here!

Malvolio, Malvolio, thy wits the heavens restore!

Endeavour thyself to sleep, and leave thy vain bibble-babble.

Sir Topas!

Maintain no words with him, good fellow!

Who, I sir? Not I, sir! God buy you, good Sir Topas!

Marry, amen!

I will, sir, I will!

Fool! Fool! Fool, I say!

Alas, sir, be patient!

I am shent^ for speaking to you!

What say you, sir?

Good fool, help me to some light and some paper. I tell thee I am as well in my wits as any man in Illyria.

Well-a-day that you were, sir!

By this hand, I am! Good fool, some ink, paper and light, and convey what I will set down to my lady.

It shall advantage thee more than ever the bearing of letter did.

I will help you to't.

But tell me true, are you not mad indeed? Or do you but counterfeit?

Believe me, I am not, I tell thee true.

Nay, I'll ne'er believe a madman till I see his brains. I will fetch you light and paper and ink.

Fool, I'll requite it in the highest degree. I prithee be gone!

I am gone, sir, and anon, sir, I'll be with you again, In a trice, like to the old Vice,^ Your need to sustain.

Who, with dagger of lath,^ in his rage and his wrath, Cries 'Ah ha!' to the devil: Like a mad lad — 'Pare thy nails, dad!'

'Adieu, goodman devil!'

ACT IV, SCENE III:
OLIVIA'S BEDROOM

This is the air; that is the glorious sun...

This pearl she gave me, I do feel't and see't...

And though 'tis wonder that enwraps me thus...

yet 'tis not madness.

Where's Antonio, then?

I could not find him at the Elephant, yet there he was, and there I found this credit, that he did range the town to seek me out.

His counsel now might do me golden service.

For though my soul disputes* well with my sense that this may be some error but no madness, yet doth this accident and flood of fortune so far exceed all instance, all discourse, that I am ready to distrust mine eyes, and wrangle with my reason that persuades me to any other trust but that I am mad.

Or else the lady's mad.

Yet if 'twere so, she could not sway her house, command her followers, take and give back affairs and their dispatch, with such a smooth, discreet and stable bearing as I perceive she does.

There's something in't that is deceivable*...

But here the lady comes!

ACT V: THE GROUNDS OF OLIVIA'S HOUSE

Now as thou lov'st me, let me see his letter.

Good Master Fabian, grant me another request.

Anything!

Do not desire to see this letter.

This is to give a dog, and, in recompense, desire my dog again.

Enter Orsino

Belong you to the Lady Olivia, friends?

Ay, sir, we are some of her trappings.

I know thee well.

How dost thou my good fellow?

Truly, sir, the better for my foes, and the worse for my friends.

Just the contrary: the better for thy friends.

No, sir: the worse.

How can that be?

That most ingrateful boy there by your side, from the rude sea's enraged and foamy mouth did I redeem.

Notable pirate, thou salt-water thief, what foolish boldness brought thee to their mercies whom thou, in terms so bloody and so dear, hast made thine enemies?

Orsino, noble sir, be pleased that I shake off these names you give me. Antonio never yet was thief, or pirate, though I confess, on base and ground enough, Orsino's enemy.

A witchcraft drew me hither.

A wrack past hope he was. His life I gave him, and did thereto add my love, without retention or restraint, all his in dedication. For his sake did I expose myself (pure for his love) into the danger of this adverse town; drew to defend him when he was beset;

where being apprehended, his false cunning (not meaning to partake with me in danger) taught him to face me out of his acquaintance, and grew a twenty years' removèd thing while one would wink; denied me mine own purse, which I had recommended to his use not half an hour before.

How can this be?

When came he to this town?

Today, my lord, and for three months before no interim, not a minute's vacancy, both day and night, did we keep company.

Here comes the Countess!

Now heaven walks on earth!

But for thee, fellow — fellow, thy words are madness. Three months this youth hath tended upon me.

But more of that anon.

Take him aside.

What would my lord — but that he may not have — wherein Olivia may seem serviceable?

Cesario, you do not keep promise with me.

Madam —

Gracious Olivia —

What do you say, Cesario?

Good my lord —

My lord would speak; my duty hushes me.

Come, boy, with me!
My thoughts are ripe in mischief.
I'll sacrifice the lamb that I do love,
to spite a raven's heart within a dove.

And I most jocund, apt,
and willingly, to do you rest,
a thousand deaths would die.

Where
goes
Cesario?

After him I love more than I love
these eyes, more than my life,
more by all 'mores'
than e'er I shall love wife.

If I do feign,
you witnesses above,
punish my life for
tainting of my love.

Ay me, detested!
How am I beguiled!

Who does beguile you?
Who does do you wrong?

Hast thou forgot thyself?
Is it so long?

Call forth
the holy
father!

Come
away!

Whither,
my lord?

Cesario! Husband! Stay!

'Husband'?

Ay, husband! Can he that deny?

Her husband, Sirrah?

No, my lord, not I!

Alas, it is the baseness of thy fear that makes thee strangle thy propriety. Fear not, Cesario, take thy fortunes up! Be that thou know'st thou art, and then thou art as great as that thou fear'st.

O welcome, father!

Father, I charge thee by thy reverence here to unfold

(though lately we intended to keep in darkness what occasion now reveals before 'tis ripe)

what thou dost know hath newly passed between this youth and me.

A contract of eternal bond of love, confirmed by mutual joinder of your hands, attested by the holy close of lips, strengthened by interchangement of your rings; and all the ceremony of this compact sealed in my function, by my testimony.

Since when, my watch hath told me, toward my grave I have travelled but two hours.

O thou dissembling cub! What wilt thou be when time hath sowed a grizzle on thy case?

Or will not else thy craft so quickly grow that thine own trip shall be thine overthrow?

111

Farewell, and take her, but direct thy feet where thou and I henceforth may never meet!

My lord, I do protest—

O do not swear! Hold little faith though thou hast too much fear!

For the love of God, a surgeon!

Send one presently to Sir Toby!

What's the matter?

He's broke my head across, and has given Sir Toby a bloody coxcomb too!

For the love of God, your help! I had rather than forty pound I were at hom...

Who has done this, Sir Andrew?

The Count's gentleman: one Cesario. We took him for a coward, but he's the very devil incardinate.

My gentleman Cesario?

'Od's lifelings! Here he is!

You broke my head for nothing; and that that I did, I was set on to do't by Sir Toby.

Why do you speak to me? I never hurt you. You drew your sword upon me without cause!

But I bespake you fair, and hurt you not.

If a bloody coxcomb be a hurt, you have hurt me. I think you set nothing by a bloody coxcomb.

Here comes Sir Toby halting^: you shall hear more. But if he had not been in drink, he would have tickled you othergates^ than he did.

How now, gentleman! How is't with you?

That's all one. 'Has hurt me, and there's th'end on't.

Sot, didst see Dick Surgeon, sot?

O, he's drunk, Sir Toby, an hour agone; his eyes were set at eight i'th'morning!

Then he's a rogue, and a passy measures pavin.^ I hate a drunken rogue!

Away with him!

ho hath made this havoc with them?

I'll help you, Sir Toby, because we'll be dressed together.

Will *you* help? An ass-head, and a coxcomb, and a knave? A thin-faced knave? A gull?

Get him to bed, and let his hurt be looked to.

I am sorry, madam, I have hurt your kinsman. But had it been the brother of my blood, I must have done no less, with wit and safety.

You throw a strange regard upon me, and by that I do perceive it hath offended you.

Enter Sebastian

Pardon me, sweet one, even for the vows we made each other but so late ago.

One face, one voice one habit, and two persons!

A natural perspective that is, and is not!

Antonio! O my dear Antonio! How have the hours racked and tortured me since I have lost thee!

Sebastian, are you?

Fear'st thou that, Antonio?

How have you made division of yourself? An apple cleft in two is not more twin than these two creatures.

Which is Sebastian?

My father had a mole upon his brow.

And so had mine.

And died that day when Viola from her birth had numbered thirteen years.

O, that record is lively in my soul! He finished indeed his mortal act that day that made my sister thirteen years.

If nothing lets to make us happy both, but this my masculine usurped attire, do not embrace me, till each circumstance of place, time, fortune, do cohere and jump that I *am* Viola.

Which to confirm, I'll bring you to a capta in this town, where lie my maiden weeds; by whose gentle help I was preserved to serve this noble count.

All the occurrence of my fortune since hath been between this lady and this lord.

So comes it, lady, that you have been mistook. But nature to her bias drew in that. You would have been contracted to a maid; nor are you therein, by my life, deceived:

you are betrothed both to a maid and man.

Be not amazed; right noble is his blood.

He's here writ a letter to you. I should have given't you today morning — but as a madman's epistles are no gospels, so it skills not much^ when they are delivered.

Open't and read it.

Look then to be well edified, when the fool delivers the madman.

BY THE LORD! *Madam!*

How now, art thou mad?

No madam, I do but *read* madness; an your ladyship will have it as it ought to be, you must allow *Vox.*^

Prithee, read i'thy right wits.

So do I, madonna. But to read his right wits is to read thus. Therefore, perpend, my princess, and give ear.

Read it you, sirrah.

By the Lord, madam, you wrong me, and the world shall know it. Though you have put me into darkness and given your drunken cousin rule over me yet have I the benefit of my senses as well as your ladyship.

I have your own letter that induced me to the semblance I put on; with the which I doubt not but to do myself much right, or you much shame. Think of me as you please. I leave my duty a little unthought-of and speak out of my injury. The madly-used Malvolio.

And, acting this in an obedient hope, why have you suffered me to be imprisoned, kept in a dark house, visited by the priest, and made the most notorious geck and gull^ that e'er invention played on?

Tell me why?

Alas, Malvolio, this is not my writing, though, I confess, much like the character. But, out of question, 'tis Maria's hand.

And now I do bethink me, it was she first told me thou wast mad. Then cam'st in smiling, and in such forms which here were presupposed upon thee in the letter.

Prithee, be content. This practice hath most shrewdly passed upon thee; but when we know the grounds and authors of it, thou shalt be both the plaintiff and the judge of thine own cause.

Good madam, hear me speak, and let no quarrel, nor no brawl to come, taint the condition of this present hour, which I have wondered at.

In hope it shall not, most freely I confess, myself and Toby set this device against Malvolio here, upon some stubborn and uncourteous parts^ we had conceived against him.

Maria writ the letter at Sir Toby's great importance^— in recompense whereof he hath married her.

121

How with a sportful malice it was followed may rather pluck* on laughter than revenge —

if that the injuries be justly weighed* that have on both sides passed.

Alas, poor fool, how have they baffled thee!*

Why, 'some are born great, some achieve greatness, and some have greatness thrown upon them.'

I was one, sir, in this interlue one Sir Topas, sir! But that's all one. 'By the Lord, fool I am not mad

But do you remember 'Madam, why laugh you at such a barren rascal? An you smile not, he's gagged

And thus the whirligig* of time brings in his revenges.

I'll be revenged on the whole pack of you!

He hath been most notoriously abused.

Pursue him and entreat him to a peace: he hath not told us of the captain yet.

When that is known and golden time convents, a solemn combination shall be made of our dear sou

Meantime, sweet sister, we will not part from hence.

Cesario, come!

For so you shall be, while you are a man; but when in other habits you are seen, Orsino's mistress, and his fancy's queen!

GLOSSARY
As shown in the text with a △

2
pitch – value

3
hart – stag
shaft – love's arrow
liver – passionate desires

4
Elysium – heaven

5
mine own escape . . . the like of him – my own escape
    gives me hope that as you say, he's also escaped

7
let her except before-excepted – she's always put up
    with it before

8
he'll have but a year – in a year he'll blow the lot
the viol de gamboys – a bass viol
natural – half-witted

9
a coistrel – a peasant
his brains turn o'the toe . . . top – he's as drunk as a
    wobbling whipping top
Castiliano vulgo – put on a straight face

10
buttery bar – liquor shelf
it's dry – dried up, impotent
dry jest – stupid jest
barren – empty (of jests)

11
canary – sweet wine
in the tongues – in the study of languages
a huswife take thee between her legs and spin it off –
    a. a housewife might use you as a distaff, (his hair
        being the flax on it)
    b. a whore give you VD so your hair falls out

12
kickshawses – antics (quelque chose)
an old man – an old hand
a galliard – a 5-step dance with a 'caper' before the fifth
cut a caper – do dance steps (capers were also used for
    mutton sauce)
back trick – (a dance step, but the image implies he's
    good in bed)
Mistress Mall – (a beautiful woman, fallen out of favour at
    court)
a coranto – a fast dance
a sink-a-pace – (a dance step, but the image suggests
    pissing in the sink)
formed under the star of a galliard – destined to dance
dun – brown
Taurus – (the 12 Zodiac signs were thought to govern
    different parts of the body)

14
nuncio – ambassador
constellation – disposition
yet a barful strife! – what an obstacle course!

15
colours – enemies
a good lenten answer – an answer meagre enough for
    Lent (a time of fasting)
let summer bear it out – it's not so bad being
    unemployed in the summer
points – points (but also suspenders)
gaskins – wide trousers
if Sir Toby stopped drinking . . . Eve's flesh – if Sir Toby
    stopped drinking so much he'd see you're as clever
    and sexy a piece of womankind as any in Illyria

16
Quinapalus – (an imaginary philosopher)

17
let the botcher mend him – let the clothes-mender patch
    him up
there is no true cuckold . . . – life's too short to lose your
    good looks over old worries
misprision – misunderstanding
cucullus non facit monachum – there's more to a monk
    than his habit (hood)
I wear not motley in my brain – I'm not such a fool as I
    look

18
doth he not mend? – (Olivia means that Feste gets more
    amusing; Malvolio interprets it as more foolish)
fox – back-stabber

19
zanies – stooges
birdbolts – arrows (i.e. mere banter)
Mercury – the god of cheating
endue thee with leasing – endow you with deception

20
pia mater – brain

21
above heat – above normal temperature
the crowner – the coroner
a sheriff's post – a wooden post outside the sheriff's
    house, symbolising authority
a squash – an unripe pea pod (peascod)
a codling – an unripe apple
in standing water – (ie: as at the turn of the tide)

22
to con – to learn
comptible – sensitive

23
If I do not usurp myself – If I am not an imposter
usurp yourself – misuse your gifts
swabber – deck-washer
hull – float about
your giant (a pun on Maria's small size)

24
such a one I was this present – this is the real me

25
the nonpariel of beauty – unequalled in beauty
voices well divulged – well spoken of

26
cantons – songs
fee'd post – paid messenger

27
blazon – heraldic coat of arms (and therefore breeding)
mine eye too great . . . mind – I've fallen in love with just
    good looks

29
malignancy of my fate – evil influence
distemper – infect
my determinate voyage is mere . . . – I've no idea where
    I'll end up

31
put your lord into a desperate assurance – make it clear
    to your master he has no hope

32
pregnant enemy – Satan
proper false – good-looking
such we be – (i.e. weak)
fadge – turn out

33
diliculo surgere (i.e. Early to bed and early to rise, makes
    a man healthy, wealthy and wise.)

34
a catch – a song
Pigrogromitus . . . Vapians . . . Queubus – (scholarly
    sounding gobbledegook to impress)
leman – girlfriend
impeticos thy gratillity . . . bottle ale-houses – (more
    mock brilliance, but containing the ideas:
    a. I pocketed your tip
    b. who gives a toss for Malvolio?
    c. Olivia is a good sort
    d. we're real men who drink real ale, so to hell with it)
testril – sixpence

35
wise man's son – fool
contagious breath – bad breath
contagious – effective, moving
dulcet – sweet
welkin – sky
draw three souls out of one weaver – (weavers were
    noted for hot gospel singing)
dog at – good at
catch – grip

37
Cataian – Chinaman, promise-breaker
politians – shrewd operators
Peg-a-Ramsey – kill-joy
Tilly-Vally! – What nonsense!
natural – naturally (also, idiotic)

38
coziers – tinkers
Sneck up! – Hang you!
ginger – (used to spice ale)

39
gull him into a nayword – make a laughing-stock of him

40
cons state – learns etiquette
the best persuaded of himself – conceited
on a forgotten matter – when we can't remember which
    of us wrote it

41
Penthesilea – Queen of the Amazons
I am a foul way out – I'm up shit creek
call me cut – useless, castrated (i.e. 'no-balls')
burn some sack – mull sherry

42
antic – quaint
recollected terms – artificial phrase

43
favour – face

44
so wears she to him, so sways she . . . – so she grows
    naturally towards him, and he finds her power over
    him acceptable
hold the bent – stand the strain
bones – bone bobbins
it is silly sooth, and dallies with – it's the simple truth and
    dwells upon

45
cypress – cypress-wood coffin
my part of death, no one so true – I am the truest lover
    who ever died for love

46
opal – (gem symbolising inconstancy)

47
give place – go away
that mirace and queen of gems – (i.e. her beauty)
pranks – adorns
cloyment and revolt – sickness and revulsion

48
Patience on a monument (allegorical figure carved on a
    tomb)
our shows are more than will – we show out more than
    we really feel
bide no denay – endure no denial

50
metal of India – gold
contemplative – staring
close! – hide!

51
affect me – fancy me
jets – struts
advanced – puffed up
'Slight – God's light

52
the Lady of the Strachy (an aristocrat who married a
    commoner)
Jezebel – poseur
blows – swells
stone bow – catapult
branchèd – richly embroidered
demure travel of regard – cool look round

53
cars – carts (and horses)

54
gin – trap
spirit of humours – eccentricity
her very C's etc. – (C, U, T, spells 'cut': the slit through
    which a woman P's)
the impressure her Lucrece – (the image shows the
    Roman woman Lucretia, who stabbed herself to wipe
    out the dishonour of being raped)

55
numbers – verse-pattern
brock – badger, stinker
sway – rule
fustian – high-falutin'
dressed – served
the staniel checks at it – the kestrel turns in mid-flight to
    swoop at it
formal capacity – intelligence
Sowter will cry . . . – (Malvolio is compared to Sowter, a
    stupid hare-hound who follows cold scent – i.e. an old
    one – even though it's obviously the scent of a fox, not
    a hare, he follows an eccentric idea even though it will
    lead him to a wrong conclusion)
faults – breaks in the scent
suffers under probation – stands up to investigation

56
simulation – puzzle
crush – force
revolve – consider
cast thy humble slough – stop acting like a servant (as a
    snake casts its skin)
tang arguments of state – resound with socio-political
    wisdom and quotations
put thyself into the trick of singularity – adopt eccentric
    mannerisms (to distinguish yourself from the herd)
alter services – change roles
champain – open country

57
wash off gross acquaintance – get rid of common
    friendships
be point-device the very man – do exactly as she
    suggests
strange, stout – aloof, firm

58
Sophy – Shah of Persia
play my freedom at tray-trip – put my freedom on the
    throw of a dice
aqua-vitae – cheap liquor
midwife – (notorious for drunkenness)
Tatar – hell

59
tabor – drum

60
cheveril – soft leather
since bonds disgraced them – now that we can't take a
    man's word without putting it in writing

61
orb – the world
but the fool should be – if a fool were not
I think I saw your wisdom there – I can see you've had
    the same idea
an thou pass upon me – if you're going to start getting at
    me
commodity – consignment
I am almost sick . . . – i.e. she's love-sick for Orsino)
I would play Lord Pandarus . . . – if this coin were mated
    with another, I'd play the go-between to mate you with
    Olivia (as Pandarus did for Troilus and Cressida)
conster – announce
out of my welkin – beyond me

62
craves – demands
like the haggard – like a wild hawk, swoop at every
    opportunity
folly-fall'n – who try to be funny
the list – the point
prevented – anticipated

63
most pregnant and vouchsafèd – receptive
all ready – (i.e. to use myself)

64
lowly feigning – affected humility
give me leave – let me have my say
under your hard construction – under your adverse
    judgement
at the stake – (i.e. as in bear-baiting with dogs)
a cypress – thin gauze
a cypress . . . hides my heart – gauze, not flesh covers
    my heart (therefore it's transparent how I feel)

65
a degree to – a stage of
not a grize – it doesn't get us any further
vulgar proof – simple fact of life

66
now I am your fool – (playing at double meanings, like a jester)
Love's night is noon – hidden love is now exposed
maugre – despite
do not extort . . . – don't let the fact that I'm courting you put you off responding to me
but rather reason . . . – but turn it round, and think how much better it is this way
deplore – report

67
'Slight! – God's light!
prove it legitimate – make good my case

68
balked – bungled
as lief be – as soon be
a Brownist – (follower of Browne, a church reformer)

69
curst – fierce
with the licence of ink – write more freely than you would speak
bed of Ware – (a famous oak bedstead, 10′ 9″ square)
gall – (oak-galls used in ink making, and 'bitterness')
goose-pen (goose-quill, and 'foolish pen')
cubiculo – cubby-hole

70
manikin to you – puppet for you
two thousand – (i.e. the money Toby has milked from Andrew)
hale – drag
the youngest wren of nine – (smallest in a nest of small birds; another pun on Maria's size)
the spleen – a good laugh
a pedant – an old-fashioned schoolmaster
the new map – (i.e. covered with new detail)

71
jealousy – concern

72
uncurrent – worthless
worth – wealth

73
for traffic's sake – merely for the sake of good relations
lapsèd – caught
the Elephant – (an inn of that name)
bespeak our diet – order our meals
your store . . . – you don't have enough to buy souvenirs

74
what bestow of him? – what shall I give him?

75
sweet Roman hand – pretty italic handwriting (and a reference to Lucrece)
yes, nightingales answer daws! – yes, I'm answering your call!

77
come near me now – do you now understand me?
sir of note – well-known gentleman
limed – caught
'fellow' – (he takes her to mean 'equal' or 'mate')
drawn in little – brought together

78
carry his water . . . – take his urine to be diagnosed (to see what's wrong with him)

79
bawcock – fine fellow (beau coq)
biddy – chicken
gravity – a dignity
cherry-pit – (children's game of throwing cherry stones into a hole)
foul collier – dirty coalman (i.e. one who gets as black as the devil)
his very genius – he's fallen for it totally
lest the device . . . – in case we're found out
bring the device to the bar – reveal all

80
the blow of the law – on the right side of the law

81
bum-baily – bailiff
let me alone for – I'm good at
clodpole – blockhead
cockatrices – (fabulous monsters that killed just by looking at their victim)

82
unchary – lavishly
that honour saved may upon asking give – that may be given on demand without loss of chastity

83
dismount thy tuck – draw your sword
yare – quick
unhatched rapier – ceremonial sword
on carpet consideration – at court
hob-nob! – death or glory!

84
conduct – safe conduct
computent – sufficient (for a challenge)
undertake that – (i.e. a duel)
meddle – get involved
to a mortal arbitrement – to the death

85
firago – warrior
a pass – a bout
inevitable – inescapable
the Sophy – the Shah of Persia
make the motion – put it to him
is as horribly conceited – has as terrifying a thought

86
for the supportance of his vow – so that his honour can
  be satisfied
duello – rules of duelling

87
an undertaker – a second

88
I'll make division of my present – share what I have on
  me

89
we'll whisper o'er . . . – we'll exchange a few flowery
  sentences ourselves

90
I my brother know . . . – I've kept alive my brother's image
  . in my own appearance
'Slid – God's eyelid
An I do not – if I don't (cuff him)

91
well held out – well kept up (their wit match)
lubber – great lout
a cockney – a wet
ungird thy strangeness – stop pretending you don't know
  me
purchase – (i.e. hire purchase)

92
an action of battery – assault case
you are well fleshed – you've had your fight

93
malapert – insolent

94
Rudesby – ruffian
extent against – violation of
started one poor heart of mine in thee – he's made my
  heart miss a beat by making yours skip
Lethe – the river of forgetfulness

96
bonus dies – good day (bad latin)
the old hermit of Prague . . . – (scholarly sounding
  references, cobbled together)

97
barricadoes – (ramparts made of barrels)
clerestories – windows
lustrous – translucent
Egyptians in their fog – plague of darkness

98
Pythagoras – the Greek philospopher
for all waters – versatile

99
perdie – certainly

100
how fell you besides your five wits? – what's made you
  lose your senses
propertied me – treated me like a senseless object

101
shent – rebuked
the old Vice – (a character in morality plays who made
  sudden appearances, and pared his nails with a
  wooden lath or dagger)

102
credit – report
disputes well – agrees
deceivable – deceptive

103
chantry by – chapel nearby
whiles – until
what time – at which time

105
and make – and thus make
as kisses – (because they bring opposites together: four
  lips together, two mouths)
double-dealing – duplicity
primo, secundo, tertio – first, second, third
the triplex is a good time . . . – triple-time is good for
  dancing

106
Vulcan – (blacksmith of the gods)
baubling – insignificant
unprizeable – not worth capturing
scathful – damaging
bottom – ship
that very envy . . . – that even his victims admired him
fraught – cargo
brabble – brawl
distraction – madness

107
wrack – casualty
face me out . . . – deny that he knew me

109
fat and fulsome – gross and distasteful
even what it please my lord . . . – do what you like
Egyptian thief – (who was prepared to kill his lover rather
  than die alone)
screws me – wrenches

111
strange thy propriety – hide the fact that you're my
  husband
grizzle on thy case – grey in you hair

112
coxcomb – head
'Od's lifelings – God's little life

113
halting – limping
othergates – in another way
passy measures pavin – piss-artist

115
nor can there be that deity in my nature – I'm not a god,
    to be in two places at once
in that dimension . . . – still in my own body

116
lets to make us – stops us being
weeds – clothes
to her bias drew . . . – made everything happen as it
    should

117
the glass seems true – what seems to be illusions
    appears to be true
orbed continent – (the sun)
in durance – under arrest
enlarge him – release him
holds Belzebub at the stave's end – keeps the devil at
    bay

118
skills not much – matters little
allow vox – let me do the right voice

119
proper cost – own expense
quits you – releases you from his service

120
the lighter people – the light-weights

121
geck and gull – fool
parts we had conceived . . . – acts we held against him
importance – insistance

122
pluck on – call for
baffled thee – made a mockery of you
whirligig – spinning top
convents – calls us together

123
wive – marry
toss-pots – drunks
When that I was and-a little tiny boy . . . etc –
    When I was a child, I got away with murder, but when I
    grew up I was really up against it: I couldn't get one
    over on my wife, and all my floozies were drunks